The Kingdom of God and the Homosexual
International Copyright © 2000 Desert Stream Ministries

Revised June 2007

All Rights Reserved

Published by Desert Stream Press
706 Main Street
Grandview, MO 64030

www.desertstream.org

This publication or parts thereof may not be reproduced in any form, stored in a retrieval system, or transmitted in any form by any means: electronic, mechanical, photocopy, recording, or otherwise without prior written permission of the publisher. The only exception is brief quotations in printed reviews.

Unless otherwise noted, all Scripture quotations are from the HOLY BIBLE: NEW INTERNATIONAL VERSION®. Copyright © 1973, 1978, 1984 International Bible Society. Used by permission. All rights reserved.

International Standard Book Number: 978-1-930159-02-0

Printed in the United States of America

Design: Immanuel Communications

Dedication

*To Mark & Gail Petterson and Christopher & Dorothy Greco
for pastoring churches in which the kingdom
moves mightily to heal the homosexual*

Introduction

We live in a highly sexualized, gender-bending age. How do we bring the kingdom of Jesus, full of grace and truth, to persons caught in the swirl of today's confusion? Consider these three faces of homosexuality.

A young adult woman, married with two small children, announced to me that she had fallen in love with a woman. She claims both she and her new partner are Christians. She is seriously considering leaving her family for a new life as a lesbian, claiming she must 'be true to herself.'

A mega-church leader, known for his traditional views, is discovered to have had a long-term relationship with a male prostitute. He is fired from his pastorate, and remains murky about the extent of his difficulties. Soon after, he claims his problem is cured after 3 weeks of "healing."

A young man confessed to me same-sex attraction. After 10 years of gay activity, he now wants nothing more than to rediscover the faith of his youth, and meet people who can help him resolve his problem. He is grateful to discover that Christian support exists for people like him who are seeking to overcome unwanted same-sex attraction.

George Eldon Ladd asserts: "In Jesus, God has taken the initiative to seek out the sinner, to bring lost men and women into the blessing of His reign." That kingdom applies as pointedly to the one struggling with same-sex attraction as it does any human being crying out for mercy. Jesus transforms broken lives, regardless of their starting point. In this way, the restoration of the homosexual is a powerful expression of the healing of all men and women.

But unlike other expressions of brokenness, homosexuality has become profoundly divisive in the church and in the world today. We polarize over questions like: Is it wrong? Is it inborn, unchangeable?

What is the role of choice, if any, for those struggling? What about those who don't struggle at all, who believe they can be fully gay and fully Christian?

Most sexual addictions and abuses are still considered immoral. But to consider homosexuality a brokenness to be restored, let alone a sin to be forgiven, invites judgment from those who hold such views as cruel and irrelevant in a society whose primary value is 'tolerance.'

In this booklet, we will consider the best ways of understanding same-sex attraction, as well as the different options available for those motivated by them. Cultural influences in this decision-making, the biblical witness, and wise pastoral and community support will be explored.

Our goal together is to manifest the kingdom of God to those seeking Jesus earnestly in light of their same-sex tendencies. How we as a community of the kingdom offer ourselves to that one will make a huge difference in his/her discovery of Jesus. Full of grace and truth, Jesus is ever faithful to manifest Himself as dynamic and relevant to the struggle at hand.

A Changing Culture

Our world now accepts a variety of sexual behaviors that would have been taboo 50 years ago, including same-sex activity. Shame used to restrain it; now the barrier of cultural has significantly broken down, as growing rates of gay behavior reveal.

Fueled by easy access to gay chat rooms and pornography on the Internet, increased heterosexual promiscuity, and the rise of divorce and multiple marriage partnerships, homosexuality today seems like one of many normal departures from heterosexual monogamy.

The media face of homosexuality is clever, hip, and sexy. In a recent survey of young men ages 14-25, nearly all had positive, even enthusiastic responses from the peers to whom they disclosed their homosexuality. There are now at least 3500 gay advocacy clubs in US public schools that confer a gay identity and lifestyle onto teens as young as 12-years-old.

Their world has become so gay-friendly that over 85% of teens with same-sex attraction claim to not want to change. Most psychological and educational associations have capitulated to gay activists that insist there is nothing wrong with homosexuality. Now struck from the diagnostic manuals as a disorder, the only problem with homosexuality, psychologically-speaking, is one's refusal to embrace his/her true 'gay' self. According to a prominent gay activist, "This is the generation that gets homosexuality. We are going to win."

Win what? Full acceptance of homosexual and lesbian activity in all walks of life—gay marriage, gay adoptions, gay-affirmation from kindergarten storybooks to university curriculums. At stake is a redefinition of monogamy; gay couplings tend to prefer 'open-style' relationships in which one may have multiple sex partners while still claiming allegiance to one person.

As social attitudes change, so do the rates of gay activity. Lesbian activity multiplied 14 times in the nineties. By the age of 30, 14% of all women reported at least one lesbian relationship, with the percentage slightly lower for men.

A Changing Church

Gay activists have mobilized in nearly every major Christian denomination as well, insisting on full acceptance in Jesus' name. The Episcopal Church is in shambles due to its gay-affirming leadership majority; the ordination of gay bishop Gene Robinson in 2003 fractured the church and sent out fissures that multiply to this day. The once conservative Presbyterians just capitulated to its gay affirming members and gave local presbyteries the right to decide questions of gay ordination and blessing same-sex unions.

The Catholic hierarchy continues to tow a hard line theologically but has failed to persuade the faithful that they practice what they preach. Since 1950, 4% of priests in the USA have abused (mostly) teen boys, roughly the same percentage of teens in the US who struggle with same-sex attraction. The sins of the fathers are in truth passed down to the children.

Emerging non-denominational groups are open to alternatives to what they perceive to be 'bad religion'. Intent on affirming the uniqueness of the seeker and allergic to appearing judgmental or abusive, many of these grass-root groups welcome practicing gays. Then gay-affirming agendas prevail. In the name of compassion, many earnest 'evangelicals' are changing their views on monogamy and sexual purity.

The Church of Jesus Christ is deeply divided over homosexuality. What the Apostle Paul described as the 'pillar and foundation of the truth' (1 Tim. 3:15) seems more confused and disoriented in her truth-bearing than powerful in it.

Among a generation who has come to believe that same-sex attraction and activity are normal and akin to ethnic diversity, we have a mandate: to demonstrate the all-surpassing power of God's kingdom. Revealed in Jesus Christ, that kingdom is able to descend into lives and reclaim them back to God's high intention for them. Our goal as His body is to seek to manifest that kingdom. He charges us to extend His transforming love to all who seek it.

We have an opportunity. The good news about today's nearly shame-free approach to homosexuality? The issues lie nearer to the surface; prodigals and quiet strugglers alike will be more inclined to convey openly their longstanding conflicts. We have answers for them. They may be unclear as to what needs to be cleansed and restored. We must be prepared to serve these ones according to the clear witness of Jesus.

Definitions

What is homosexuality? Let's look first at same-sex attraction. These are feelings of sexual and/or emotional desire for one's own gender. The onset of these feelings is usually in late childhood. Tendencies arise and may create conflict for the struggler. Here we must distinguish between desires that are unwanted, and a host of other attachments that one can make later in light of those desires. At this point, let us refer only to the attraction itself.

Here we are dealing with a deep-seated conflict tied into one's identity as an emerging man or woman. The road to gender clarity is a hard one. Though God intends for each person to realize mature heterosexuality, one can get stuck and cease progressing onto wholeness. Boys must achieve some sense of masculine empowerment, optimally through an engaging father. Girls are more subject to abusive treatment at the hands of men, and may fail to enter into a secure feminine identity. Destabilized by trauma, some women may view men as a threat, not a gift, and seek refuge in the consoling arms of other women.

Two factors then may be at work in the pre-teen facing same-sex attraction: a disempowered sense of personal gender identity, as well as a distorted view of the opposite-sex. Approximately 1.5-3.5% of the US population possesses same-sex attraction at this young age.

Multiple Influences

I do not mean to simplify what can be a complex and profound network of desires; the route to mature heterosexuality may also be influenced by prenatal hormones, family-of-origin, generational patterns, birth order, and temperament. Still, what is nearly universal in the preteen struggler is a perception of gender inferiority. A yearning for same-sex attention and affection arises out of this perception of inadequacy. It is as if one is seeking through his/her newfound sexuality to repair what is damaged, to complete what is not whole.

Robert Gagnon in his superior book The Bible and Homosexual Practice writes: "This is not a healthy reaching out to the 'other' but rather a narcissistic attraction…a symptom of an unmet need for sexual self-acceptance."

If that is true, then to bless those tendencies as one's sexual destiny is to block the goal of sexuality: heterosexual maturity. Rightful interpretation of same-sex attraction is crucial; we must ask—what do the desires mean? This allows all involved, including caregivers, to take these desires seriously, without doing damage to the struggler. And what damage is being done in the name of justice and tolerance by confirming the (pre)teen as a gay adult!

Moral Decisions

This is where the greater environment and culture makes a huge difference. Habitual use of pornography, counsel/mentoring that is gay-affirming (often from media gurus), and sexually active relationships empower same-sex desire and persuade the teen that (s)he is destined for a gay identity and lifestyle.

We are witnessing a proliferation of gay behavior among teens. Researchers at Johns Hopkins University remarked at the influence of gay-saturated culture upon US youth. They write: "Sexual identity unfolds during the teen years and is influenced by sexual experience and the 'acquired tastes' closely related to the culture in which the individual develops…it is possible to picture a future in which gay behavior will be so much a part of every individual that any deeper contribution (e.g. genetic, psychological) will be undetectable."

In other words, those with same-sex attraction will be matched by those looking for a new thrill without the motivation of a deeper 'attraction.'

This is where Jesus commands His church to call young men and women into a higher standard for sexual identity and behavior based upon His kingdom. Jesus entered into the lives of broken people with a love so powerful that one had to make a decision about who (s)he would follow: Jesus or other objects of desire. Ladd describes one requirement of the kingdom of God: "Any tie or human affection which stands in the way of one's decision for the kingdom of God and Jesus has to be broken."

Kingdom Decisions

Choosing Jesus in light of one's same-sex attraction is a spiritual choice that has profound moral implications. Such 'kingdom' decision-making will impact his or her identity, behavior patterns, and lifestyle.

Same-sex attraction does not necessitate that one identifies as a homosexual or a lesbian. The gay-affirming world seeks to confer that label immediately, making a tendency the center of one's identity. Jesus, on the other hand, wants to confirm the struggler as a child of God and break the claim of homosexual identity upon him or her.

The same applies to homosexual behaviors. Simply having a desire for something in no way implies that such desire must be satisfied. Every individual possesses a multitude of feelings that one learns to negotiate in terms of what (s)he views as wise and true. The gay-affirming world encourages offering oneself and his/her tendencies to a variety of sensually pleasing behaviors; Jesus wants to be the sole object of one's worship, and Lord over what one does with his or her body.

Finally, the gay-affirming world wants humanity to make life decisions according to these behaviors. That means that homosexuality begins to determine one's entire social sphere. Jesus, on the other hand, is intent on creating a people who make decisions for their lives based on His righteousness and holiness. Jesus wants to be the Lord over one's lifestyle, and displace one's sexuality as the basis for one's social destiny.

Jesus brings His kingdom to fallen humanity, even and especially to those motivated by same-sex attraction. He gives them the power of choice. That is not a simplistic choice to rid the self of certain feelings. Rather, one can decide in light of those feelings to be defined by Jesus, and to allow Him to determine one's course.

Grace and Truth

Jesus commands His community to manifest His kingdom to those with same-sex attraction. As Jesus embodied both grace and truth (Jn 1: 14, 17), so must we. All persons possess a longing for unfailing love. Our churches can be places of welcome for those seeking that love—to begin to receive 'living water' from the gathered people of God. In light of many different starting points, individuals should have ready access to discover God's love in His community; Christ through His body has power to satisfy what no one person of either gender can offer another.

Jesus exemplified this advance of disarming grace in His response to the Samaritan woman in John 4. She was cut off from 'religion' due to shame tied into her ethnicity, her gender, and especially her sexually immoral state. As such, she typifies the kind of sinner who is genuinely surprised to discover that God loves her. Jesus engages with her artfully at Jacob's Well, offering her a type of water that He claimed had power to quench her thirst forever.

Similarly, our churches can be a gathering place where the famished discover real spiritual food and drink. We must make a way for those hungry in their same-sex attraction to discover Jesus' love among us. As water upon dry ground, this love awakens a deeper cry for fulfillment that transcends sexual yearning. It lays the groundwork for a sinner's response of committed love to Jesus and His Kingdom.

Jesus fused grace with truth, and so must we. After offering her 'living water,' Jesus asks her to call her husband. After she stammers a bit, He makes clear that He knows of her many ex-husbands and of her current lover. In so doing, Jesus reveals the truth of her deception. She is drawing from a fountain of carnal love that cannot satisfy her. In grace, Jesus offers her a better way, and in truth, He reveals the false and inherently frustrating course she is on.

He also invites her into her highest and truest self—one who was destined to worship God. Perhaps she would join the ranks of those who having received His Kingdom would then "worship the Father in Spirit and in truth" (Jn 4: 23). The entire passage is a prophetic; it reveals a glimpse of how Jesus' Kingdom love breaks through layers of sin and shame and lays claim to one's true identity and destiny. He does this to establish us in the only love that can actually satisfy the deepest longings of our hearts (Eph. 3: 16-19).

Clarity of Truth

On what basis did Jesus determine the Samaritan woman's sin? We must determine truth for the strugglers in our midst. That is essential. The world and the worldly church have a different basis for determining sexual morality. For them, feelings become one's self-definition and right to act. Today's culture defines sexual morality in terms of: 'I feel, therefore I am, and I must act.'

Seekers will come to us in powerfully influenced and motivated by this standard. We cannot afford to be naïve or unclear as to the way of Jesus, the truth that counters us in order to fulfill us.

As pastors and counselors, we must represent Jesus. He sees beneath the seeker's immediate hungers. He seeks to satisfy the deeper cries for intimacy—the longing that only He as God can satisfy in human hearts. He also holds to a higher view of who the person actually is destined to be in relation to others. In other words, Jesus may lovingly interfere with how we feel and think about how we meet our needs for love. He invites us into His kingdom, under His loving rule, and helps us to aspire to what is best and true.

Jesus and the Image of God

Jesus spoke authoritatively of His intentions for humanity in Matthew 19:4-6. He said: "Haven't you read that at the beginning the Creator made them male and female, and said 'For this reason a man will leave his mother and father and be united to his wife and the two will become one flesh'? So they are no longer two but one. Therefore what God had joined together, let not man separate."

Jesus anchors our understanding of God's intentions for our gender and our sexuality in Genesis 1 and 2. He takes us back to Eden in order to grasp His will for our humanity—who and how we are to be in relation to each other.

Our understanding of what is broken and what is best must first be rooted in what is good about our sexual humanity. The Father graced His human creation with the distinct call to bear His image. Among other things, 'image-bearing' involves the fullness of male and female together (Gen. 1:26, 27).

Scripture then reveals more of this fullness in Genesis 2. Adam's longing 'to not be alone' (v.18) conveys an inspired emotional and physical drive in humanity for partnership with the opposite gender. Later in that chapter marriage is ordained. There sexual love flourishes within the boundaries of committed heterosexual love; it is the only ordained context for erotic love in scripture. Sex seals a togetherness found on intellectual, emotional and spiritual levels between these two very different creatures.

In their gender 'otherness,' intimacy is intensified. And growth occurs as marital love calls each out of what is familiar to his/her own gender and into discovery of the other's difference. That points to the goal of our adult sexual development: desire for the other gender based on clarity in one's own gender, as well as the call to mature in faithful love of this other in light of and in spite of our feelings.

Gender complementarity—the reality that God ordained humanity as part of His heterosexual creation—is a window to God's holiness, or 'otherness'. God is different from us. He is holy, distinct from those

He created. Yet He sets His image and likeness into humanity as 'male and female.' That human image mirrors Him in the differences between male and female. We reflect an aspect of His holiness to the degree that man and woman together are joined in honorable submission to one another in their gender differences.

Just as God calls us to worship Him in His otherness, so He calls us to manifest Him on earth through whole heterosexuality. His 'otherness' is revealed in our honoring the 'otherness' of the opposite gender. To tamper with the intrinsically heterosexual dimension of our creation is to defy His holiness and one of its manifestations on earth: the biblical mandate to work out our salvation together 'as male and female.'

Homosexuality in Context

What then is going on with those who long for intimacy with their own gender? That longing expresses the underlying need to be reconciled to one's own gender. Same-sex attraction implies that the struggler is only one half of his own gender. So we treat the person with dignity, a part of God's heterosexual creation who nevertheless possesses a profound brokenness.

Same-sex attraction does not negate God's will for him or her, sexually-speaking. It simply means that we must help them to resume the journey toward whole heterosexuality, with compassion and clarity. That clarity commands we exercise the biblical mandate that pursuing homosexual unions is not an option. The holiness of God is at stake. To support same-sex unions is an inexcusable rebellion against God's design for His human creation. That is why Paul uses the homosexual practice as a prime example of idolatry—of humanity's rebellion against God's holiness (Romans 1:16-32).

But Paul also states in Chapter 2 of Romans that those aghast at homosexual idolatry should take heed in light of their more subtle but no less grievous sins. He reminds the readers that "they too are without excuse in light of their judgments"; they have fallen similarly, and have forgotten "that God's kindness led them into repentance" (vs. 1-4) in the first place.

Same-sex attraction, as well as its misdirected expression in gay acts, must be understood in context. Both are woven into the fabric of a fallen, idolatrous culture. In this way, we do well to return to Genesis in order to grasp the greater heterosexual crisis out of which homosexuality emerges as one expression of disorder.

Genesis 3 reveals the awful and immediate impact of sin upon gender and sexuality. Man and woman lose sight of God and a clear view of one another. Under the curse, as a consequence of sin, woman longs for man inordinately and man rules over her with frustration and strife. (vs.16-19) Traditional sins issue out of that broken image as readily as water from a cracked pipe. All manner of broken boundaries, including sexual abuse and addiction mark the broken image, not to mention emotional hostility between the sexes and severed commitments. Most of this is entirely heterosexual.

Out of this legacy of relational sin, the potential for gender-bending tendencies arise. Dishonor between men and women breaks ground for more exotic expressions of gender brokenness; homosexuality emerges out of fallen heterosexuality. Consider these cultural realities:

- In the sixties, we challenged marriage as the context for sexual expression, and disassociated sex from commitment.
- In the seventies, we challenged marital commitment. We instituted 'no-fault' divorce and serial monogamy.
- In the eighties, we took pornography out of seedy downtown areas and brought it home, first through VCRs and then computers. Virtual prostitutes became the drug of choice for a generation weaned on the Internet.
- In the nineties, idolatrous heterosexuality extended its authority over gay rights and acts. Bill Clinton became the first US president to advocate the normalizing of homosexuality in the USA, the same decade that saw an unprecedented leap in gay behavior.

Sexual and Relational Brokenness at the Cross

In order to impart the kingdom with clarity and justice to the same-sex struggler, we must realize how pervasive the broken image is in our culture and in our churches. God's best for His human creation remains—gender complementarity, and sex within the boundaries of heterosexual marriage.

But all have fallen short in myriad ways. In wanting to address the homosexual question well, we would be wise to first recognize the far more deadening impact of pornography, sexual abuse, divorce, and just plain heterosexual cruelty among our congregants.

Then, at the cross, we could readily make room for the smaller percentage facing same-sex attraction. We could say with authority: "Sin has shaken all of our worlds, influencing attitudes, emotions, and desires that have distorted God's image in us, and that tempt us to distort that image in others."

That is the basis for any church calling the homosexual or lesbian to repentance. Our lack of authority is based on the truth that we have tolerated 'normal sins' and 'scapegoated' more exotic ones.

One pastor recounted his conversation with a gay couple whom he was exhorting to break up for the sake of the kingdom. "You are not asking me to change hair color or to stop smoking," pleaded the one man. "You are asking me to die!" "That's right," replied the pastor. "You have not asked that of anyone else in this church; don't start with us," replied the other. The two walked out and never returned.

The point should be clear. Make sure that our commitment to redeem homosexual brokenness is integrated well into the greater call to redeem the broken image in humanity.

Kingdom Wisdom from the New Testament

Foolish exegetes claim that Jesus said little about holiness and nothing about homosexuality. He did not exclude anyone; He was the essence of tolerance, and did little more than seek solidarity with sinners. Surely His kingdom did not rock their worlds!

To be sure, Jesus said radical things like "the prostitutes will enter heaven before the Pharisees." (Matt. 21:31) He was well-aware that professional religious ones often failed to recognize their need to be saved, while prostitutes, aware of their brokenness, were more apt to cry for mercy than the pious.

But we cannot overlook the fact that Jesus made radical repentance a condition of the kingdom. He regarded all sexual activity outside of marriage a sin—not only in action but also in thought. (Matt. 5:27-30; Mk. 7:21-23) He took the Pharisee's legalism and transformed it, making impurity of heart grounds for exclusion from the kingdom altogether!

According to scholar Robert Gagnon, "Jesus took sexual sin very seriously…What was distinctive about Him was His incredibly generous spirit toward those who had lived in gross disobedience for years. He expended enormous amounts of energy and exhibited great compassion in His search for the lost…Jesus' ministry proves that the church can practice radical love without sacrificing God's demand for righteous conduct…Whenever mercy or righteousness are sacrificed, we proclaim a false Gospel."

Paul picks up these themes of mercy and truth in the context of sexual sinners who were transitioning into the church out of paganism.

Unlike Jesus whose greatest adversaries were Jewish legalists, Paul battled pagan idolatry, often expressed in grotesque acts of sexual immorality. New converts to the churches of the Greco-Roman world bore the mark of sexual addiction to either gender. Often these addictions resulted from pagan feasts in which gods and goddesses were worshipped through temple prostitutes.

The good news was that many were becoming Christians. The pastoral challenge? To curb the sexual excesses that marked their previous religion. To do so, Paul asserts the power of intimacy with the Father, as well as a command to flee the darkness of idolatry. He implored the Corinthians: "What agreement is there between the temple of God and idols? 'Touch no unclean thing, and I will receive you. I will be a Father to you, and you will be my sons and daughters,' says the Lord Almighty." (2Cor 6:16-18)

In his first letter to the Corinthians, he places homosexuals in the context of many other violators. He wisely asserts a new identity in Christ as their defining characteristic then implores them to act accordingly. He reminds them that those defined by these sins will not enter the kingdom of heaven.

"Do you not know that the wicked will not inherit the kingdom of God? Do not be deceived: Neither the sexually immoral nor idolaters nor adulterers...nor homosexuals nor thieves nor slanderers ...shall inherit the kingdom of God. And that is what some of you were. But you were washed, you were sanctified, you were justified in the name of the Lord Jesus Christ, and by the Spirit of God." (1Cor. 6:9-11)

Repentance

Paul implored his young flock to identify with Christ and so cast off the old restraints that marked their lives of sexual brokenness and sin. This implies they had the time and opportunity to actually get to know this God who was asking them for everything. That is key. Often we command repentance from those who don't actually know Him. That takes time—a lot of community, a lot of convincing and softening and breaking off deception through unfailing love—the community of the kingdom.

We need to provide that context of holy love and acceptance in which these ones can make a choice: who shall I serve? Then, at the right time, according to pastoral wisdom and discernment, we call him/her to respond to Elijah's challenge. The prophet commanded a people divided in their spiritual allegiance to make a choice. "How long will you waver between two opinions? If Baal [a Canaanite fertility god worshipped through sexual excess] is god, follow him. If Jahweh is God, follow Him." (1 Kings 18:21)

That means responding to the challenge. And making a choice. No one can choose for another. And we need to prepare for the fact that many will not choose Jesus but rather the gods and goddesses of the gay affirming world.

Those who choose Jesus must count the cost. That cost involves giving up gay lovers, as well as addictive sexual patterns. It means letting go of homosexuality as the basis for one's identity and life-style. Jesus gave everything for us and asks for everything from us. In dying to the 'old man,' one receives Jesus as the basis for the new creation. And just as the gay community may have provided solidarity for the nourishment and support of the gay self, so must the community of faith make very effort to fortify the Christian emerging out of the grave clothes of his/her homosexuality.

This is a community affair. When Lazarus was raised form the dead, he still bore the mummification of his dead self. Jesus commanded those around him to help remove the bandages, one layer at a time (Jn 11:44). This requires time and patience. We do well to encourage the one risen with Christ to choose Him continuously. (S)he will be sustained by the Risen King as the community does its part.

Deeper Healing

But what about the same-sex attraction itself? How does one overcome such desire and actually begin to think and feel according to his/her new status as part of God's heterosexual creation?

One needs several things in order to go deeper in the healing process. Let's begin with reasonable expectations. It is unrealistic to expect same-sex attraction to go away quickly. That is because the feelings express a need for love and identification with one's own gender. Jesus does not heal our needs; rather, He helps us to meet them the right way. Obviously, gay relationships and identity are not the answer. But neither is denial of the need for connection with one's own gender. That connection is a normal part of development that the struggler failed to realize in childhood.

Same-sex attraction indicates an effort of the soul to compensate for its deficits. That deficit involves two parts. The first is an emotional rupture, or injury in relation to the same-sex parent. That injury provoked a defensive mechanism that prevented the child from rightfully identifying with his/her own gender. Behind that defense, the child remains immature, unable to grow into adequate gender wholeness.

Same-sex attraction is a distorted expression of a normal emotional longing for connection and identification with one's own gender. That need has become perverted. But the need must be reclaimed from its perversion and handled uprightly and forthrightly by the one bearing that need. We do a disservice to those struggling with same-sex attraction to dismiss the real needs underlying the sexual desire.

Healing then involves three parts. The first is identifying the injury, the point of shutting down in relation to one's own gender. Often we have made vows against the same-sex parent or authority figure. We may have blocked and countered what we perceived to be shaming or harmful in those relationships. Yet in detaching from that figure, we may have blocked our own development.

Healing involves identifying that breakdown. It is no small matter, and should involve wise and consistent healers who can skillfully help the struggler identify the injury, feel appropriate pain, forgive the offender, and begin to let go of vows related to his/her gender.

The second part of the healing takes longer; it involves learning to relate whole-heartedly with one's own gender. That is difficult, as one may feel a variety of conflicting emotions, like sexual longing, anger, frustration, and loneliness. But a solid community of faith can provide a sound context in which the struggler can begin to resume this key aspect of his/her journey onto wholeness.

Given the commitment to Jesus and His kingdom, as well as to solid supporters around him or her, one can face fears tied into same-sex relating. I compare it to walking onto ground that feels uncertain, even treacherous. But with the help of Jesus and wise walking partners, one can walk through the myriad emotions and temptations. Out of this process, subject to progress and regress, one realizes (s)he can secure same-sex friends that are free from lust and fear. And deeply fulfilling without being perverse!

The shaky ground hardens as one walks on it; likewise, the struggler begins to grow solid within. One begins to make peace with one's gender, to accept oneself in relation to God and others as a whole-enough man or woman. That is no small achievement, given the damage done and the time lost. Still God is faithful, and makes a way for His creation to be reconciled to God's best for him or her.

On that basis, one begins to feel ready for heterosexual relating. One realizes that same-sex friendship is only the first step to discovering the whole of God's creation. One must go into the land of the 'other' in order to realize what it means to bear God's image. A community of the kingdom, founded on Jesus and His grace and truth, is solid ground on which the struggler can take first steps here.

Marriage is not the goal. One need not marry in order to experience and rejoice in heterosexuality. Image-bearing involves the breadth of life: church, mission, vocation, neighborhood, and friendship. The whole of community life involves participating in the duality of male and female. Recognizing the difference, and realizing with new eyes and heart that one is a gift to the 'other' and actually needs the other's offering as well—that is heterosexual wholeness.

God is faithful. He sends His kingdom to us in Christ. He asks us all to give Him everything, whether our starting point is homosexual or not. He is faithful to reconcile us to His best for us. That is the kingdom: the birth of new possibilities—new life.

A wise man writes: "God's kingdom is the power of God. It is the revelation of the divine life on earth. It is the birth of new hearts, new minds, and new feelings. That is the kingdom. Jesus has laid the foundation for a completely new life, a new order. In Him we have become completely different men and women in the very depth of our beings."

Preparing the Church to be a Kingdom Community

The healing of the homosexual necessitates a healing community. Relational problems require relational solutions. One is wise to consider the values and practical steps necessary to create a healing content for those with same-same attraction.

One must count the cost. We live in a consumer-driven culture. And have fashioned consumer-driven churches. That means we tend toward low-hurdle, low-cost approaches to seekers. That is good to an extent. Isaiah prophesied the flood of mercy initiated by the Messiah when he said: "Come, all you who are thirsty; come to the waters; you who have no money, come buy and eat. Come buy wine and milk, without money and without cost. Why do you spend money on what is not bread, and your labor on what does not satisfy? Listen to me and eat what is good, that your soul may delight in the richest of fare." (Is. 55: 1, 2)

In truth, the kingdom is a free gift. On the other hand, one cannot partake of its riches unless (s)he is willing to forsake false food, and then find support for developing new eating habits. As we have seen, that is usually an extensive process for the same-sex struggler.

So a congregation must count the cost. Will its free gift to seekers also include a rather intensive and rigorous follow through for those in need of it? In my experience, congregations most successful at 'catering' to seekers often do not want to invest much in reversing the bad eating habits of the saved.

Put another way, the healing journey is nothing short of a discovery of the cross—the dynamic and often mundane journey of dying to what is less in order to live more fully to what is right and true. It can be messy. It is always lengthy. And in the case of the homosexual, it is controversial. The cross is costly. A free gift that demands all—first from the individual, and then from the community that surrounds him or her.

The church must answer the question: are we willing to raise hard issues, like homosexuality and the greater brokenness that surrounds it? Many seeker-sensitive churches have gone on record as saying that they won't stir the waters with hard issues; they simply let God take care of them. That is theologically false and irresponsible. God's kingdom comes through His community. Naïve churchmen who leave such work to mysticism join in the silence of the shamed and make room for false agendas. Fools rush in when the church does not address clearly the brokenness of its members.

Facing the Offense of the Cross

The truth is: the cross drives a stake through our consumer-driven sensibility. It is disruptive. The bloody God-man refuses to be soft peddled. These are some questions to ask yourself and your congregation:

Is your church willing to include people who are offensive? That means individuals bearing the mark of gender brokenness and rebellion—people at odds with themselves and often proud it. Most people are normally offended by homosexual seekers. Their brokenness sets them off, and makes them uncomfortable.

Equally, many are offended by a clear and proactive approach to restoring the homosexual. Usually due to unrepentant family members, these ones will squirm at any notion that homosexuality is both a disorder and a sin. That offends the post-modern mind. *Will you run the risk of scattering some in order to redeem others? Are you willing to stand firm in the face of those who oppose you?*

Is your church willing to catch a glimpse of its own brokenness— that of the breadth of the broken image—in the face of the same-sex struggler? That is key. Authority to restore the homosexual hinges upon the entire congregation reckoning with the greater relational mess that surrounds same-sex attraction. That will require thoughtfulness and time from the pulpit.

Having taught on the relevant biblical topics, resulting in corporate repentance, *will the church provide the time, space, and grace for the process of healing to occur?* That means sponsoring a healing group like Living Waters (will discuss this later) as well as working in conjunction with solid Christian therapists.

Healing the homosexual exposes hearts: it reveals the Laodiceans in your midst who like the Pharisees refuse to reckon with their brokenness and repent (Rev. 3: 14-18); at the same time, it will provoke the Thyatirans who follow the teachings of Jezebel by affirming the sexually immoral, using false notions of justice and mercy (Rev. 2:20-25).

Will you allow the kingdom of Jesus in your church to heal and divide? A wise man writes: "If we truly love Jesus, we will love everything in Him, not only His compassion and mercy, but His sharpness too. It is His sharpness that prunes and purifies...Christ's love is not the soft love of human emotion but a burning fire that cleanses and sears."

Practical Steps to Bringing the Kingdom to the Homosexual

We face an amazing opportunity in our culture. As brokenness and perversion grows in the land, so will a moral dullness that fails to even flinch at new expressions of darkness. This is the church's shining hour! This is our opportunity to get ready and receive those whom God has prepared to enter His kingdom. "Multitudes, multitudes in the valley of decision; the day of the Lord is near in the valley of decision." (Joel 3:14)

Intercession

I would urge you to rally the intercessors in the church. Like Nehemiah, we can rightfully assess the grave disrepair of God's image in humanity, both in the world and in the church. "You see the trouble we are in: Jerusalem lies in ruins, its gates burned with fire. Come let us rebuild the wall of Jerusalem, and we will no longer be in disgrace." (Neh. 2:17)

Make that rebuilding the focus of prayer. Pray for the release of captives. Pray for the mercy and truth of Jesus to be established in your community. Pray for salvation, and for healing opportunities for those in such disrepair.

One good focus of prayer is repentance unto healing. That can be the repentance of the sin-weary, or those priests like Daniel who represent the fallen and repent, using the corporate 'we.' (Dan. 7: 17-19 is a good example of this.) A wise man writes: "Just as there is a momentum to evil, so there is a momentum to repentance; to reprove perversion, we must repent of lust, to turn from infidelity, we must renounce divorce and impurity."

Preaching, Teaching, Testimonies

Prayer lays the base for solid teaching and preaching, particularly the brokenness and restoration of the broken image in humanity. Especially helpful for the church are the testimonies of men and women who have walked through significant brokenness into wholeness. Objective teaching about homosexuality is well-complemented by members of the church who give a face to overcoming same-sex issues.

Such testimonies are significant for all involved; they are not to be taken lightly. One must be ready for such a declaration. When (s)he is prepared, a way is made in the wilderness! People in the church will come out of the woodwork when they hear the courageous voice of an 'over-comer'. Desert Stream Ministries exists because my pastor urged me to share my testimony one Sunday morning nearly 30 years ago. How much more relevant is that word today!

Releasing Evangelists, Preparing Healers

Many in your churches are already engaging with same-sex strugglers every day of their lives: at work, at home, at school. The way to share Jesus with them is no different than anyone else; His offering of tender mercy is free and able to satisfy one's deepest desires. And His powerful love demands a truthful choice—who will one serve? Hopefully your community is becoming a watering hole that gives the seeker a fighting chance to decide.

Gifted evangelists bring in seekers then the healers come into play. These are the men and women who have gone deep with God in their own weaknesses and who now want to comfort others as they have been. (2Cor 1: 3-5) A wise pastor with a heart for the sexually broken will not try to do the hard work on his/her own. The process is far too intensive for one priest. It must be carried by a team of wounded healers under his/her auspice who can walk the broken into wholeness.

Living Waters and CrossCurrent

We have found the best way to restore the sexually broken is through small groups. If well-run and implemented, that group can impart a depth and breadth of healing beyond what one-on-one meetings can do. Also, the weight of the process is not on one person; it is shared by a team. What can be the intense and complex dynamics of individual counseling is offset by a community of healers. That also satisfies legal concerns. Churches need not be rocked by liability suits if tough issues are handled in the light of several witnesses.

Living Waters is an in-depth, 30 week approach to the healing of homosexuality, as well as other sexual and relational issues. We have found that same-sex attraction is best worked out amid a range of other problems like (hetero) sexual addiction. A community of same-sex strugglers is usually not healthy. One needs to understand the same-sex struggle in the light of diverse struggles. In this way, (s)he is challenged to see his issue as one common to humanity, and in the group to take his/her place among the whole.

Please read the chart at the back of this booklet entitled 'Mature Heterosexuality.' This may help one to see how Living Waters seeks to impart the kingdom to same-sex strugglers through the group process. It is a combination of Spirit-filled prayer facilitated by the community, paired with key insights from reparative and developmental psychology. At every point, we place our hope in Jesus, that His Presence would enable participants to progress into maturity as we learn to rightfully trust Him and His community.

CrossCurrent is an 8 week group that prepares people for the deeper healing offered in Living Waters. It is easier to run and evangelistic in nature. It is a good offering for a church to begin with in its effort to restore the sexually broken. Both groups require that its leaders undergo a 6-day intensive training sponsored by Desert Stream Ministries, which also provides the curriculum and standards for the group.

Small Groups and Authority in an Age of Deception

Having these gathering points is crucial to the kingdom hope you are extending to the sexually broken. It grants you authority as a church to proclaim genuine, practical hope for those seeking Jesus and His kingdom in their struggle. These are the groups that you as a church are saying: "This is the way; we urge you to walk in it!"

Having a healing track gives you recourse for those who refuse to get any help. Those who say they want help but then fail to do anything about it are without excuse. They limit their own involvement in the church due to their unwillingness to humble themselves and to gather with others on the journey toward wholeness.

Same-sex strugglers run the risk of encouraging same-sex attraction in themselves and others unless they choose to get healing. This requires an effort. It means getting real with inner desires and the increasing temptations of a gay-friendly world. The struggler either gathers to solidify core foundations of the soul, or refuses to do so. Those who refuse run the risk of self-deception and imparting that deception to others.

Local leadership teams must provide a clear, united front for those strugglers in the church who refuse to get help. The good news? There is a way forward. The bad news is when individuals refuse the help and thus exclude themselves from greater community involvement. Assign blame where blame is due. It helps broken people when they take responsibility for their own poor choices.

Proclamation and Pastoral Care

Making a way for individuals with same-sex attraction to receive healing is a prerequisite for upholding a standard of righteousness for the greater community. We must first ensure that our wounded are being cared for. Then we can proclaim from our pulpits the need to restrain gay marriage initiatives, etc. Issues of social justice and morality must be preceded by justice in our churches.

We first humble ourselves before God as the broken image-bearers that we are. We care for those with same-sex attraction in our midst. God's image is being raised up in our midst. Then we have authority real to counter the growing deception in the land.

I love Jesus' version of justice as prophesied by the Isaiah: "I [the Father] will put my Spirit on Him and He will bring justice to the nations. He will not shout or cry out or raise His voice in the streets. A bruised reed He will not break, a smoldering wick He will not snuff out. In faithfulness He will bring forth justice." (Is. 42: 1-4)

May our churches be agents of Jesus' justice; we do so by providing powerful pastoral care for those with same-sex attraction. May our social proclamations be founded on that expression of justice: His kingdom restoring bruised, flickering lives.

Gay Christians?

A misnomer from the start. But a growing threat in the evangelical/charismatic church. There is a strong and assertive minority in the conservative church that insists one is born gay, cannot change, can practice gay sex, and still be true to the God of the Bible. Though obviously deceived, this is a force that will continue to assert its claims upon the church until the church concedes.

This is the same strain of rebellion and perversion that fought hard in the mainline Protestant denominations and won; now it has leaped over the fence into our camp. Resist this lovingly and firmly. Do not engage in endless dialogue with this deceived point-of-view. It has been around for centuries and is only broken through repentance and the blood of the lamb.

Again, the good news is that we have an offense: the glorious kingdom that Jesus brings to same-sex strugglers. Those who will bend the knee to Him will not be disappointed. Those who assert falsehood in Jesus' name must be refused for the sake of the whole.

Growing Darkness, Greater Light

The culture is growing darker. At its core is a false and pernicious 'tolerance' that demands of Christ's body: "Unless you accept practicing homosexuals unreservedly, you are a church of hate!" Don't buy into the rhetoric. To disagree with such bad logic is actually an expression of love. Robert Gagnon writes: "There can be no transformation for homosexuals as long as they live in a world of unreality that includes false notions about scripture's view of homosexuality."

The kingdom requires truth-in-love, combined with practical and powerful resources in your church for those ready to get serious with Jesus and His people. I have witnessed amazing expressions of how Jesus has used His whole healing team in the local church—intercessors, evangelists, preachers, pastoral caregivers, and servant-hearted friends—to impart the kingdom powerfully to same-sex strugglers.

As a result, I am privileged to know hundreds of men and women formerly dominated by same-sex attraction who have now taken their places as true disciples of Christ in their churches—they have become the healers, the prophets, the teachers, intercessors, pastors, and evangelists. This occurred as each submitted his/her same-sex attraction to Jesus and His community.

Having allowed this deep move of His kingdom in their lives, they now have become oaks of righteousness that really do display the Lord's splendor (Is. 61:3); in truth, they are a glorious reflection of God's image in humanity, reclaimed through the One who manifests that image perfectly.

A few years ago, God gave me a little word with big meaning. He said: "Homosexuals will divide the church. But ex-homosexuals will heal it." I believe this word because I behold its evidence all over the world.

I count myself among this healing army. Having died to the gay self, now raised with Christ, we shall go forward with kingdom authority to proclaim the power of His love. In that love, many gays who have stood as enemies of the cross will bow the knee to Him, and be restored as Jesus reclaims the most real and true aspects of their humanity. Together we will labor to prepare a pure bride for our soon-coming King.

"Now get up and stand on your feet. I have appointed you as a witness of what you have seen of me and what I will show you... I am sending you to open their eyes and turn them from darkness to light, from the power of Satan to God, so that they may receive forgiveness of sin and a place among those who are being sanctified by me." (Acts 26: 16-18)

Mature Heterosexuality

Living Waters provides a healing track for resuming the journey onto mature heterosexuality. Its goal is to identify blocks on the path, begin to remove them, and to equip participants to engage rightfully with others in order to achieve mature heterosexuality. Resuming the journey is a gift of God's Kingdom revealed to humanity through Jesus Christ. Living Waters relies constantly on God's intervention along the natural therapeutic course in order to unblock or accelerate that journey in extraordinary, inexplicable ways.

Key insights from the reparative view

- Whole gender formation and mature heterosexuality are achievements, not "natural states".

- Classic homosexuality is a breakdown in relation to one's own gender. Its healing must involve addressing core wounds with same-sex parent, undoing the detachment, and securing sources of same-sex love rightfully.

- This will involve facing ambivalence towards one's own gender: frustration, anger, fear, longing, and lust.

- The Living Waters group will facilitate a variety of "natural" transferences that begin to reveal this ambivalence: the wounding, defenses and unmet needs at the core of homosexuality.

- The group will help the participant resume the journey toward wholeness, but in no way promises to complete it. Our intention is to significantly unblock the path and empower the pilgrim to walk it.

MATURE HETEROSEXUALITY

Significant developmental stages

- 13-18 years: homosexual identity formation (gay relationships, community, sensibility)

- 13-15 years: erotic transitional phase (affectional hunger becomes erotic)

- 5-12 years: latency period (gender non-conformity, mystique of same gender, peer alienation)

- 4 years: critical role of father (evidence of defensive detachment, signs of gender disturbance, pre-homosexual/lesbian condition)

- 3 years: establishment of gender identity (autonomous identity formation/ child's awareness of gender)

- 2 years: security established/disrupted through maternal bonding

- 0-6 months: critical maternal bonding period

Contact Information:
To contact Andrew Comiskey or Desert Stream Ministries about Living Waters or CrossCurrent:
Desert Stream Ministries, 706 Grandview, MO 64030
(816) 767-1730 • info@deserstream.org • www.desertstream.org

Suggested Resources:
The Bible and Homosexual Practice *by Robert Gagnon*
The best all around book on homosexuality and Christianity. Gagnon approaches the topic from many angles with a fusion of hard intellect and inspired mercy. Available at www.robgagnon.net

Straight and Narrow (InterVarsity Press) *by Thomas Schmidt*
A solid, comprehensive book on homosexuality from a Christian perspective. Schmidt takes on theological issues involving God's intent for sexuality, "Christian" pro-gay rhetoric and arguments, nature/nurture issues and more. Available at **www.ivpress.com**

Homosexuality and the Politics of Truth (Baker Books) *by Jeffrey Satinover*
An excellent clinical resource covering genetic influences and homosexuality, environmental causation and other nature/nurture issues. Satinover is a psychiatrist with sophisticated understanding of genetics and neurology, and is able to make the material understandable for the scientifically challenged. Available at **www.bakerbooks.com**

The Broken Image (Baker Books) *by Leanne Payne*
From the standpoint of inner healing, the best book on the healing of the homosexual. Available at **www.bakerbooks.com**

Pursuing Sexual Wholeness (Creation House) *by Andrew Comiskey*
The author uses his testimony and those of others to relate how Jesus used the church in the healing of each one's homosexuality. Available at **www.dspress.net**

Strength in Weakness (InterVarsity Press) *by Andrew Comiskey*
The author broadens the scope of sexual and relational brokenness here, and describes the healing power of the cross in the community as key to restoring the breadth of such brokenness. Available at **www.dspress.net**

What Helps?
Confessions of a Homosexual Struggler in the Church

1) I need to share openly and honestly about my same-sex attractions. I feel rotten about it but my shame and silence only makes the struggle worse. I need to confess it as well as any sinful expressions of my tendencies, to a trustworthy person like you. Your words of forgiveness, encouragement, and acceptance are milestones in my healing..

2) Your acceptance of me in light of my struggles begins to break down the lie that I'm a worse sinner than most, more deserving of judgment than the next guy. Your support helps me to believe that Jesus is my Advocate. I'm beginning to see that Jesus draws near to me in my weakness in order to empower me; He doesn't detach from me and expect me to get better alone. Thanks for being available sometimes too, and helping me to see that healing is a process.

3) Because these feelings are strong in me, and because at times I really want to give in, I need the truth of what's right and wrong. I don't need the Bible thrown at me; I do not need clarity from Scripture about my sexuality. Don't treat me differently from anyone else. You challenged me when you said sexual boundaries apply to everyone, regardless of their tendencies. I wanted an excuse and you called me to be responsible. I hate that but I need it.

4) It helps me to understand that my same-sex feelings contain an underlying message about my need for security and confirmation as (wo)man. That makes sense to me. I've always felt inferior in relation to my own gender. That insight helps me to refuse the sexual aspect of my struggle but to accept the truth that I need healthy and supportive friendships with other (wo)men.

5) Thanks for treating me like a Christian friend and not a "homosexual." You've helped me to believe the truth that my real identity is in Christ and in His community. You also prayed for me to receive the Father's blessing as a (wo)man. That really helped me. The Holy Spirit is taking more and more ground in my heart.

6) Thanks for extending the hope of healing to me. For the first time I feel like I've got a relational future that could even include heterosexual intimacy. Thanks also for directing me to that Christian counselor and to Living Waters. Between that specific help, and my involvement in the church, I'm on a solid track to becoming the (wo)man God created me to be.

Andrew Comiskey

NOTES: